Text: Isidro Sánchez
Drawings: Vincenç Ballestar
Illustrations: Jordi Sábat
Editorial direction: José M. Parramón Homs
Translation: Edith V. Wilson

© Parramón Ediciones, S.A. 1992
Published by Parramón Ediciones, S.A. Barcelona, Spain

The title of the Spanish edition is *Mis primeros pasos en . . . dibujo*.

All inquiries should be addressed to:
Barron's Educational Series, Inc.
250 Wireless Boulevard
Hauppauge, New York 11788

Library or Congress Catalog Card No. 92-18320

International Standard Book No. 0-8120-1374-3

Library of Congress Cataloging-in-Publication Data

Sánchez Sánchez, Isidro.
   [Mis primeros pasos en dibujo. English]
   Drawing : Isidro Sánchez ; drawings, Vincenç Ballestar ; illustrations, Jordi Sábat].
      p.   cm. — (I draw, I paint)
   Summary: Introduces basic techniques and principles of drawing, such as proportion, perspective, and shading.
   ISBN 0-8120-1374-3
   1. Drawing—Technique—Juvenile literature.   [1. Drawing—Technique.]
I. Ballestar, Vincenç , ill.   II Sábat, Jordi, ill.   III. Title.   IV. Series: Sánchez Sánchez, Isidro.   I draw, I paint.
NC730.S275   1992
741.2–dc20   92-18320
                                                                        CIP

Printed in Spain
2345   987654321

I draw, I paint

drawing

**The materials, techniques, and exercises
to teach yourself to draw**

BARRON'S

What is...

The art and technique of drawing

This book, which is a part of the series *I draw, I paint*, teaches you how to draw. If you already can draw, the information presented will help you improve your drawing skills.

Through many practical exercises you will become familiar with the techniques of drawing and will learn how to work with the appropriate materials and accessories.

Since this book deals with drawing as an art, it will also reveal the basic artistic principles you must learn if you want to draw well. Knowing these basic principles is very useful for working with other media—including watercolors, crayons, and tempera—which you can learn from other books in this series.

Graphite pencils of varying hardness, charcoal pencils or sticks, and chalk of various colors are a few of the materials you can use to draw.

Basic drawing principles

The following is only a brief description of the three basic principles that govern the art of drawing. In subsequent pages you will find a detailed explanation of each, along with corresponding exercises that will help you put them into practice.

- **Form.** This word refers to the shape of a model—the figure, object, landscape, and so on. You must first try to draw the basic geometric shapes—squares, rectangles, cubes, circles—of your model. Such a drawing is called a *form sketch*.

- **Dimensions and proportions.** Any subject will have certain *dimensions*—that is, width, height, and depth. Generally, you will draw smaller than your subject's actual size. But whether you work larger or smaller, you must capture the *proportions*—the correct relationship of your subject's actual measurements. The way to accomplish this is by first learning how to "see" your model to determine its main dimensions.

- **Perspective.** Look at the objects around you. They are not flat, but have volume. *Perspective* helps you create an illusion of volume or depth on the flat surface of the paper.

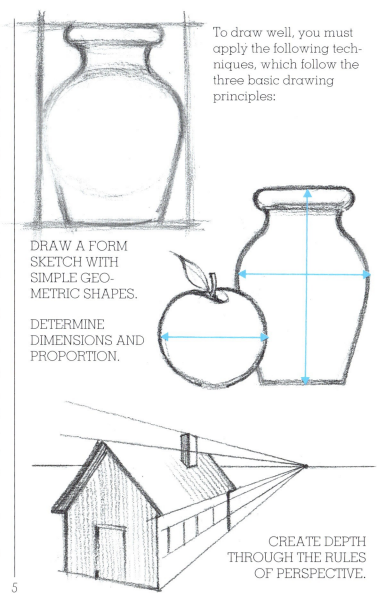

To draw well, you must apply the following techniques, which follow the three basic drawing principles:

DRAW A FORM SKETCH WITH SIMPLE GEOMETRIC SHAPES.

DETERMINE DIMENSIONS AND PROPORTION.

CREATE DEPTH THROUGH THE RULES OF PERSPECTIVE.

5

What I draw with...

Graphite pencils

A graphite pencil is simply a common lead pencil.

As you know, pencils consist of a cylindrical core, called lead, and a wood casing.

You might not know that pencil leads combine *graphite* (a black, lustrous form of carbon) and *clay* (an earthy material composed of fine mineral particles) and that the varying proportions of these substances determine the degree of hardness or softness of the leads.

The very hard pencils are used only in detailed or mechanical drawings. A medium grade can be used for most other drawing, and a soft or very soft grade for filling in large areas with light or dark shading.

The grade of a pencil is indicated by a code of letters and numbers: H is hard, B is soft; HB and F are both a medium grade. With some brands of pencils it is possible to recognize the grade by the thickness of the core; the thicker the core, the softer the pencil.

To obtain a wide range of tones, from intense black to a soft gray, you need several pencils of various grades. A basic collection of pencils includes the following grades:
- HB (to set down the first lines of a drawing)
- 2B (to produce medium tone effects)
- 6B (to create the dark tones)

From left to right: View of the inside of a graphite pencil, a mechanical pencil, and wooden pencils of various hardnesses with demonstrations of the line derived from each one.

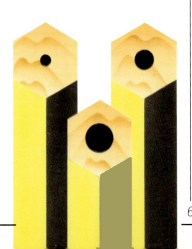

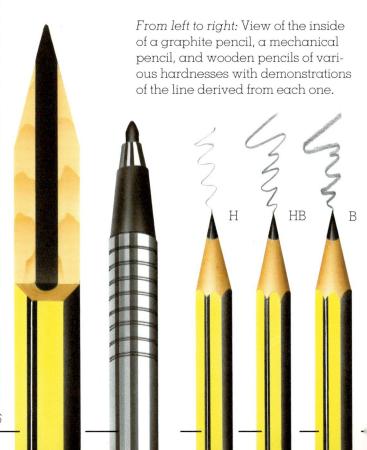

H   HB   B

Charcoal

Drawing charcoal is black porous carbon obtained from burnt wood.

Charcoal is sold in sticks of various thicknesses. You can draw with it by holding the stick in your fingers or by using a holder, which is not a widely used accessory.

Charcoal pencil

Like the graphite pencil, the charcoal pencil has a wood covering, but its core is made of compressed powdered charcoal mixed with other materials. The charcoal pencil, which can be sharpened, provides a more controlled line than a charcoal stick.

Oil or wax chalks

Chalk mixed with oil (conté crayon) or wax (lithographic crayon) is available in the form of small bars or pencils; both forms come in white and in a range of colors.

Sanguine chalk

Sanguine is the name given to a brick-red oil or wax chalk, which comes in stick or pencil form.

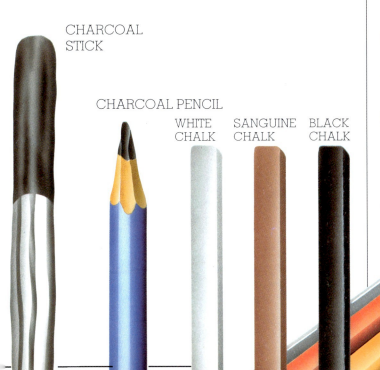

CHARCOAL STICK

CHARCOAL PENCIL

WHITE CHALK

SANGUINE CHALK

BLACK CHALK

In this illustration you can also see chalk bars in sanguine and other colors.

A BOX OF COLORED CHALKS

What I draw on...

Drawing paper

You may think that any paper is good for drawing pictures. This is partly true; but to get the best results, use paper that is specifically made for drawing, even if it is of ordinary quality.

Drawing paper is sold in pads and single sheets of various sizes.

One pad, two pads, three pads . . .

You need to start with a 14 × 17-inch (about 35 × 45 cm) pad.

Use this pad to do all of the drawing exercises in this book.

Later, when you are ready to draw on your own, you will want to buy a second, smaller pad to use as a *sketchbook*—the pad where you keep your notations and rough drawings, or *sketches*. Your larger pad should be reserved for "finished" drawings.

One advantage of paper in pad form is that your drawing will be protected after you have finished it.

Types of drawing paper

An important feature in your selection of drawing paper is its texture—that is, the coarseness or smoothness of its surface—usually referred to as "grain."

Paper is available in a variety of surfaces. You can buy grainless or glossy papers and papers with fine, medium, or coarse grain.

- With graphite pencils, smooth, glossy papers, although sometimes used, are not appropriate; the surface does not evenly accept the graphite from the pencil point. The best surface for graphite pencil drawing is a fine-grain paper.

- With charcoal or chalk, glossy papers are even less suitable. You can use a fine-grain paper, but medium-grain or coarse-grain are best.

As shown in the illustrations to the left, you need to have a special pad, or sketchbook, in which to make notes and preliminary sketches.

Look at the different results obtained by drawing these lines on (A) coarse-grained paper; (B) medium-grained paper; and (C), on glossy paper: with graphite pencil of soft (1), medium (2), and hard grade (3); with sanguine chalk (4); with charcoal (5); and with charcoal pencil (6).

What I draw with...

The work surface

There are only two requirements for the surface on which to work: The paper must rest on a flat surface that is not too hard.

It is also desirable that your work surface be slanted. The slant can be improvised with a simple drawing board.

Buy a smooth wooden board, about 18 × 24 inches (about 50 × 70 cm). When drawing, you can rest the board on your lap and lean it against the side of a table.

Metal spring clip and thumbtacks

If you draw on a loose sheet, the drawing paper must be fastened to the drawing board. You can use a metal spring clip to secure large sheets to the board or use thumbtacks—one at each corner—to fasten small pieces of paper to the board.

A large folder

A portfolio large enough to hold your biggest drawings and unused sheets of paper will be a useful accessory.

WOODEN DRAWING BOARDS

THUMBTACK

PORTFOLIO

These are some of the accessories you need for drawing.

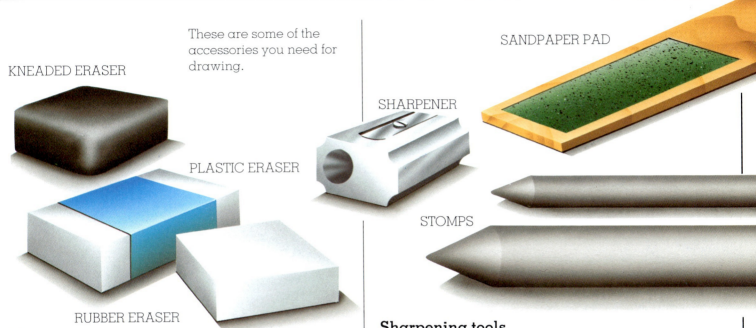

KNEADED ERASER

PLASTIC ERASER

RUBBER ERASER

SHARPENER

SANDPAPER PAD

STOMPS

Erasers

Of course, erasers are mainly used for erasing, but they can also be used for "drawing"—strange as this may seem to you now, throughout this book you will see how this can be so.

There are three types of erasers:

- Ordinary soft rubber erasers, which are very suitable when working with graphite pencil.
- Plastic erasers for more difficult erasures.
- *Kneaded erasers*, which are similar in consistency to modeling clay, are used for charcoal, conté, and soft pencil.

Sharpening tools

Some sharpening tools—such as a single-edge razor or knife—can be dangerous. For this reason, we recommend that you use a pencil sharpener; for an even sharper point, use a sandpaper pad.

Rolled paper stomps

Artists use stomps to spread and blend charcoal and chalk by rubbing it on the paper surface. Stomps come in several thicknesses.

How I draw...

The right way to hold the pencil

Grip the pencil firmly, but not too tightly. You want to draw with a loose and relaxed hand, without stiffness. This is the most common way to hold the pencil, both for sketching or developing details.

Another good way of holding your pencil is with the back part of the pencil inside your hand. This position is appropriate for drawing more freely or to obtain wide strokes.

LEAD FLAT FOR WIDE STROKES

LEAD ON POINT FOR FINE LINES

Stroke width

The broadness of the stroke depends both upon the thickness of the lead and the angle at which you place the point of the pencil on the paper.

In the illustration above you can see how the line width varies in accordance with the position of the pencil.

To outline the main forms or develop detail in your drawing, hold the pencil as you normally would for writing.

This is the best way to hold the pencil to draw broad strokes when darkening or shading large areas.

Practicing your strokes

Start with the easiest part, the pencil strokes. A stroke is a mark or line drawn on the paper. Here are the basic rules to keep in mind:

- You must complete a stroke all at once, without lifting the pencil off the paper. The line must show no interruptions but look smooth and flowing.
- Don't press the pencil hard against the paper. As you know, it is better to use a softer pencil to get a dark tone.
- Your strokes must look sharp and clean; don't retouch or go over your strokes a second time.

Types of strokes

A drawing needs different types of strokes: short and long, straight and curved, thick and thin.

Regardless of stroke type, the drawing technique is always the same: draw uninterrupted and crisp lines with confidence, as already explained. And, because no technique can be perfected without practice, keep practicing with exercises similar to the ones on this page.

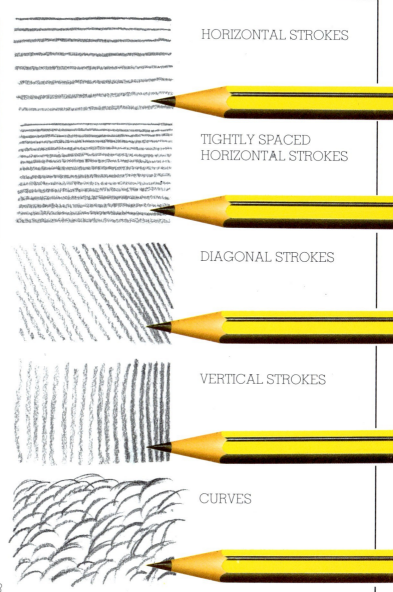

HORIZONTAL STROKES

TIGHTLY SPACED HORIZONTAL STROKES

DIAGONAL STROKES

VERTICAL STROKES

CURVES

How I draw...

Creating evenly gray tones

A uniform gray can be achieved by pencil strokes that are applied with unvarying pressure on the paper.

Draw a 4 × 4-inch (10 × 10-cm) square and then fill it in evenly with a 2B pencil. Make closely spaced diagonal strokes, trying to keep the same pressure on the pencil and going right-to-left with a flowing hand movement.

Creating a gradation

You can get a *gradation*—a gradual shift in grays—with the following technique:

As before, draw a square; now begin your strokes with a 2B pencil. At first, apply some pressure on the pencil and decrease the pressure progressively until your pencil barely touches the paper.

Now, practice another gradation: start with an HB or other medium pencil and end with a soft pencil, like a 2B.

Left: A uniform gray. Apply even strokes, maintaining a constant pressure on your pencil.

Right: A gradation achieved with two differently graded pencils: (A) The base strokes were made with an HB pencil. (B) The gradation was then created with a 2B pencil.

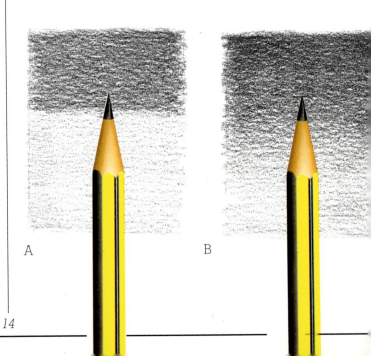

A

B

Creating uniform grays and gradations with your fingers . . .

A finger can be very useful for blending or spreading the graphite over the paper to obtain uniform grays or gradations.

You can rub the paper with a fingertip, the side of a finger, and even with the heel of a hand.

The pressure must be slight and constant.

. . . and with a stomp

How do you produce uniform and graduated grays with a stomp? Here is the technique:

- Rub the paper using only *slight pressure* on the stomp.
- Move the stomp in the *direction* of the stroke you are working on—horizontal, vertical, curved, or other.

Drawing with erasers

You can also "draw" with an eraser. That is, you can create highlights by removing grays with the eraser.

Gently rub the eraser over the area you want to lighten or highlight.

These illustrations show you the blending technique, with both a stomp and a finger, for achieving a gradation of grays, as well as the highlighting technique.

PENCIL STROKE

STROKE BLENDED WITH A FINGERTIP

BLENDING WITH THE STOMP IN THE DIRECTION OF THE STROKES

HIGHLIGHTING

How I draw...

The strokes

Charcoal does not lend itself to drawing fine lines. But you can get relatively crisp lines if you sharpen your charcoal by rubbing it lightly over sandpaper, although the point will not last long.

Give your charcoal stick a *beveled* point—that is, angled point—and you will be able to draw both fine and broad lines. By holding the charcoal upright, the line will be thin; slant the charcoal to draw heavier strokes for creating uniform grays or gradations.

As you did with the pencil, regulate the pressure of the charcoal against the paper to obtain lighter or darker grays with your strokes.

Using a protective sheet of paper under your hand

Drawing with graphite pencil, but more so with charcoal sticks or charcoal pencils, requires you to protect your drawing from smudging.

Always work with a sheet of paper under your hand, and change it when it becomes too soiled.

Strokes drawn with charcoal: (A) with the tip of the beveled point. (B) with the broad part of the beveled point. (C) with the stick on its side.

When drawing with charcoal, place a protective sheet of paper under your hand, as you see below.

Charcoal pencils

When drawing with charcoal pencils, keep these characteristics in mind:

- Charcoal clings stubbornly to the paper.
- Charcoal marks are difficult to erase.

In finished drawings, charcoal, whether from sticks or pencils, must be fixed to keep it from smudging. You can buy a *fixative* spray in any art supply store.

Erasing techniques

Charcoal can be partially removed from the paper with either a kneaded eraser or a piece of cloth, but it is not possible to erase charcoal marks completely.

However, with the eraser—or even with a finger—you can lighten and reduce tones.

Charcoal pencil and stomp technique

If you make a gradation with a charcoal pencil and then try blending with the stomp technique, you will see the tones darkening as you push the tiny particles of charcoal together.

To succeed, you must start with very few pencil strokes, which you then rub with the stomp.

TOO LONG A GRAY SECTION

BAD GRADATION

SHORT GRAY SECTION

With charcoal—sticks and pencils—you must apply very few strokes and then use the stomp to do gradations.

CORRECT GRADATION

How I draw...

Dimensions and proportions

To draw the model—a landscape, a figure, or any object—you must transfer to the paper the measurements of the subject. The dimensions of all objects in the drawing must relate proportionately to the subject and to each other.

Before beginning your drawing, look at your subject and mentally calculate its dimensions: How high is it? How wide? What basic shapes does it have?

Here is a useful measuring technique:

With a pencil in hand, extend your arm toward the subject without bending your elbow. Then move your thumb up and down the pencil until it matches the dimension of one of the elements of your subject. Now move the pencil to a second element and compare—is it larger or smaller?

You will frequently find that the measurement of each element differs. Comparing them will help you determine the dimensions and proper placement of all of the elements of your drawing.

Calculating the dimensions will help you sketch. Here, the height of the vase is equal to the total width of the elements, and the width of the apple is the same as the width of the vase top.

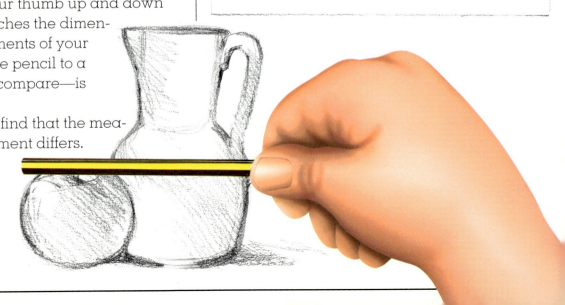

The grid

If you want to copy an image to scale, draw a grid over the photograph or drawing. Then draw a similar grid on your paper.

Done? Now you can draw, using the grid as a guide. (You are always free to vary from the source—if you choose to do so.)

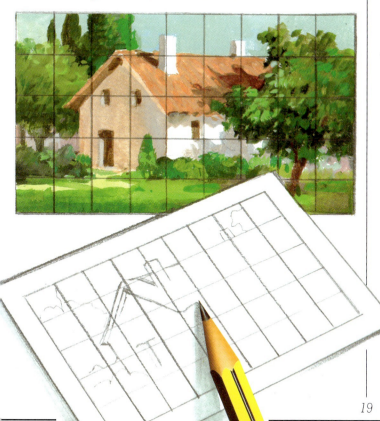

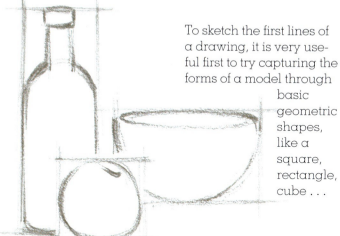

To sketch the first lines of a drawing, it is very useful first to try capturing the forms of a model through basic geometric shapes, like a square, rectangle, cube . . .

Form sketch

How should you start drawing? Begin by sketching the basic geometric shapes you see in your subject.

Keep in mind, however, that these basic geometric forms will never exactly coincide with the forms of your subject. The form sketch is actually a drawing technique for setting down the preliminary outlines of a drawing, the guiding lines that will help you begin to draw.

Look at the examples on this page; next, select some objects of your own and try to imagine which geometric shapes they might fit.

How I draw...

What is perspective?

The surface of the paper you draw on is flat—that is, it has only two dimensions: length and width. As you know, however, real objects have volume, which has a "third dimension": depth.

The rules of perspective help you create an illusion of volume, or the third dimension, on the flat paper surface.

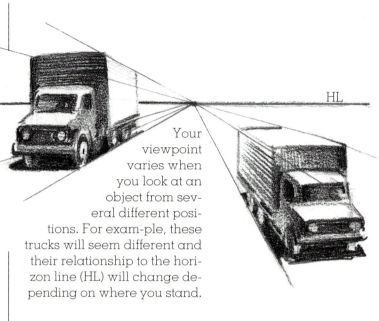

Your viewpoint varies when you look at an object from several different positions. For exam-ple, these trucks will seem different and their relationship to the horizon line (HL) will change depending on where you stand.

The basic concepts

Although the rules of perspective are complex, there are certain basic concepts that you can apply to your drawings.

Suppose you are outdoors looking at a house; you can stand directly in front of the house or move to the right or left of it. The place where you, the observer, are standing is the viewpoint.

Another basic concept is the horizon line (HL). Read the illustration captions and study the drawings on this page.

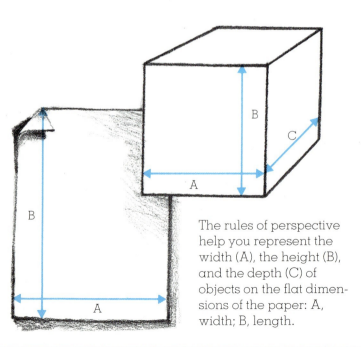

The rules of perspective help you represent the width (A), the height (B), and the depth (C) of objects on the flat dimensions of the paper: A, width; B, length.

Types of perspective

There are three types of perspective:
- Parallel-line perspective or one-point perspective
- Oblique-line perspective or two-point perspective
- Aerial perspective or three-point perspective

The vanishing point is a place on the horizon line where the lines of a drawing meet.

In parallel and oblique perspective, the vertical lines of the drawing are always parallel to each other. The rest of the lines—all horizontal—meet at the vanishing point (or points).

You will use parallel and oblique perspective most frequently in your drawings.

Aerial perspective—which you would encounter when viewing, for example, a building from a position below or above the building—has a third vanishing point where the vertical lines of the drawing merge.

Use geometric shapes to practice.

The rules of perspective are easier to see when applied to geometric figures. But it is important that you practice as much as possible. Use the figures on this page.

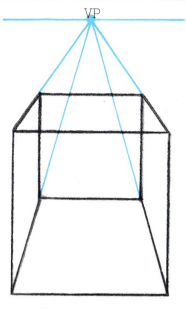

PARALLEL PERSPECTIVE

In parallel perspective, the receding lines—which are drawn by lengthening the sides of the cube and are later erased—meet at a single vanishing point (VP).

In oblique perspective—when you view an object from a position off center—there are two vanishing points; in the cube below, the receding lines on each side meet at a different VP.

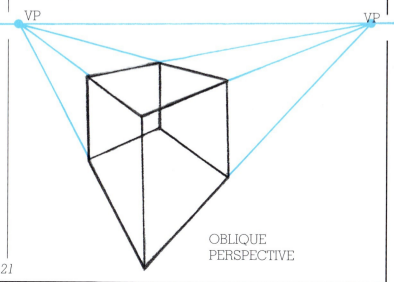

OBLIQUE PERSPECTIVE

My first exercises...

In your first exercise, you are going to practice drawing with simple geometric shapes. Sketch this flower using different ovals for the rose and its leaves.

Now try to draw the forms; outline and finish shaping the leaves and develop detail in the rose. Then determine the shadows with a few parallel strokes.

Intensify the shadows with parallel strokes, showing the forms with the stroke direction.

Continue developing details with a 2B pencil and draw your strokes more lightly or more heavily, and closer together or further apart to get a wide range of grays.

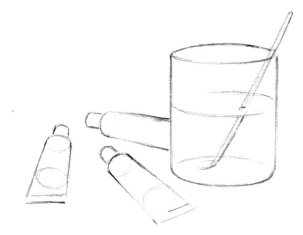

Make a form sketch of this drawing. Since the tubes of paint and the glass container are not flat, you need to draw the circles within them to give them volume.

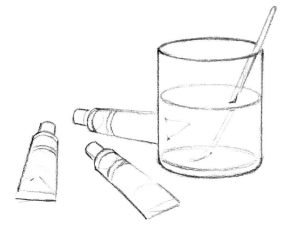

Rework the lines to give them more definition. Add some detail to the tubes and define the shadows and highlight areas of the glass jar.

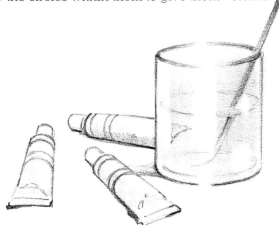

Work in a uniform gray, without pressing hard on the pencil and with strokes that follow the forms. Next, use an eraser to create the highlights on the glass container.

Now with a soft pencil develop the dark areas. Press harder to create the shadows and gradually ease the pressure toward the middle and the edges.

My first exercises...

Now here is an exercise in charcoal pencil that will make you proud. You can certainly do it if you are willing to try. The shape of the eagle's head is not difficult and, as you can see, takes only some basic strokes.

Work in an even tone of gray using parallel strokes and applying only slight pressure on the pencil. Draw first in one direction and then cross your strokes with others in a different direction. The cross-strokes will darken the tones.

This part of the exercise requires you to blend the strokes either with a finger or a stomp. Work carefully because charcoal spreads very easily. Be especially careful when you blend the beak and the area above the eye.

As a last step, develop contrast in some areas: the open beak, the eye, and the plumage. Stroke these spots over and over with the charcoal pencil. Is your eagle as spectacular as this one?

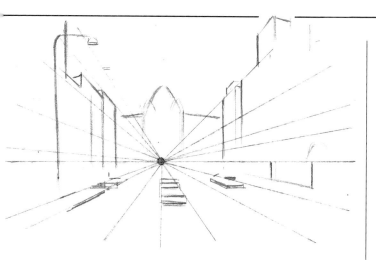

This is a perspective exercise. Draw the basic outline, then locate the horizon line and the vanishing point.

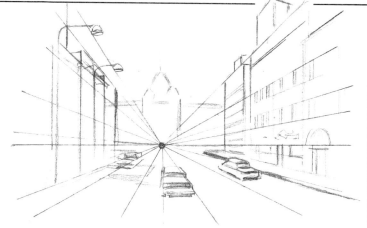

If necessary, use a ruler to be sure that all the horizontal lines intersect accurately.

Add a uniform gray cast. Direct all your strokes toward the vanishing point.

Make the shadows in the foreground stronger than those in the background. This will help you create depth.

My first exercises...

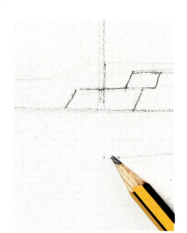

A rectangle is a good basic shape to set down the form of the boat's hull.

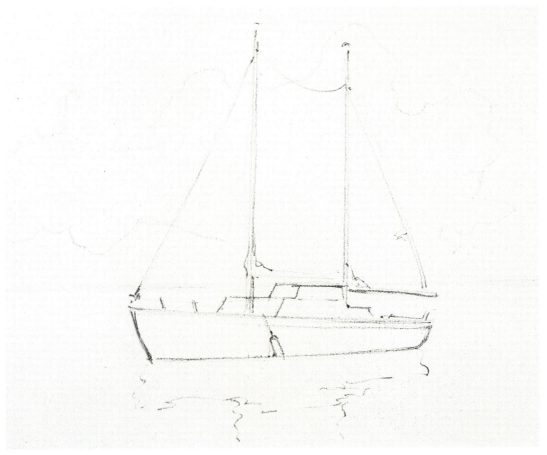

Here is an easy drawing with graphite pencil.

In this drawing the stomp technique is not required; it is entirely developed with parallel strokes.

First sketch the basic outline—the shape of the sailboat—but put in other details, such as the horizon line, the clouds, and the reflection of the boat in the water.

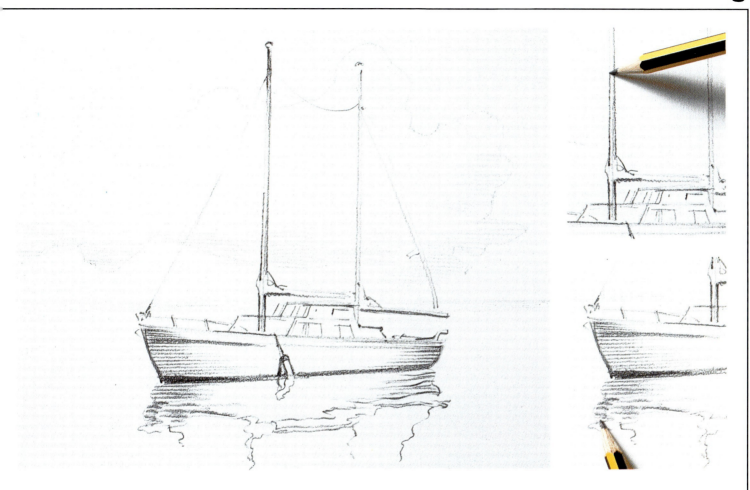

After drawing the outline, you can give more definition to lines depicting the outside of the boat's hull and the masts.

Now draw some parallel strokes in the clouds. Make them light gray by barely touching the pencil to the paper.

Darken the hull and the reflections in the water, but gradually lessen the pressure on the pencil as you work.

My first exercises...

Reinforce the outline to bring out details, like the cabin's windows.

Continue adding detail. Fill in the area of the gathered sails between the masts with very strong, slanted, parallel strokes.

Also draw a few lines in the cabin's windows, but make them lighter.

Add some background strokes—with only slight pressure on the pencil—in the reflections of the boat in the water.

Draw the waves throughout the bottom part of the picture.

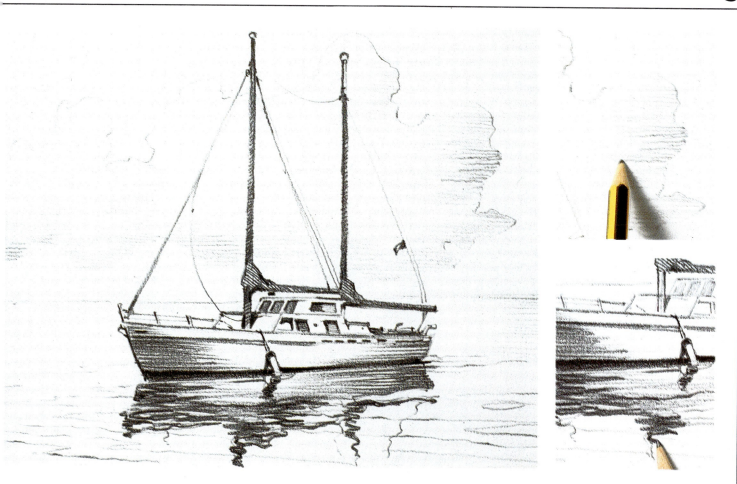

Here, work on contrast.

Create soft shadows in the clouds, but build up to a darker gray in some areas.

Do the same in the cabin's windows. Work a gradation on the boat's hull and the water reflections, spacing the strokes close together for the shadows and wider apart for the light tones.

My first exercises...

When drawing the outline, try to pick out the basic geometric forms. For example, the plane's fuselage has the shape of a cylinder.

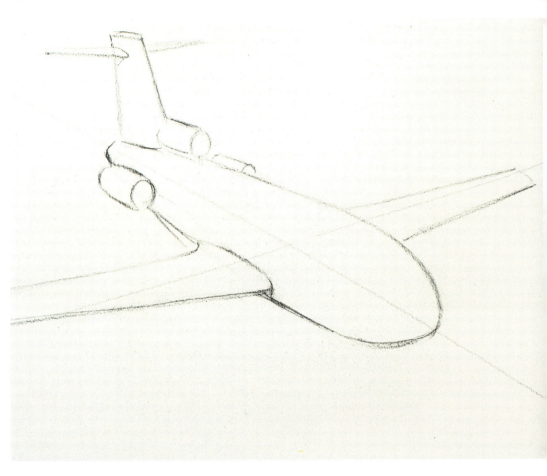

Here is another exercise for graphite pencil, but now you will blend with the stomp and your finger.

Draw two perpendicular lines on the paper, within which you will set the direction of the fuselage and the wings.

Now use an HB pencil to outline the drawing.

The motors have a cylindrical shape, as does the fuselage. Both wings have the form of an incomplete triangle.

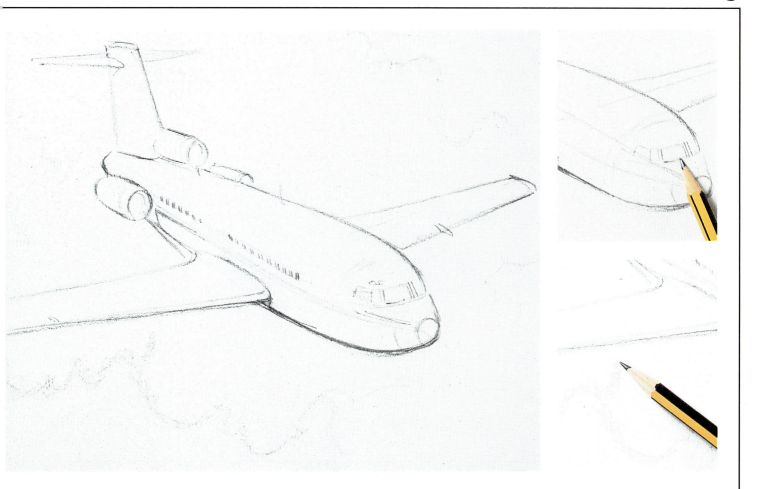

Rework the lines of the drawing with a 2B pencil.

In doing this, try to correct the forms you had previously outlined for the purpose of positioning the drawing on the paper.

Begin to put in all the details.

Draw the windows and correct the shape of the plane's nose.

Also, add the shape of the clouds.

My first exercises...

Do a gradation, as you learned in the previous pages, applying greater and lesser pressure on the pencil.

Now, use the gradation technique to add the shadows.

With the broad side of the pencil point flat against the paper, cover the background with soft strokes; apply even pressure on the pencil.

On the wings, draw some parallel strokes; on one of the wings, space the strokes close together.

Do the same on the fuselage, but work the tones of the nose to get a darker gray.

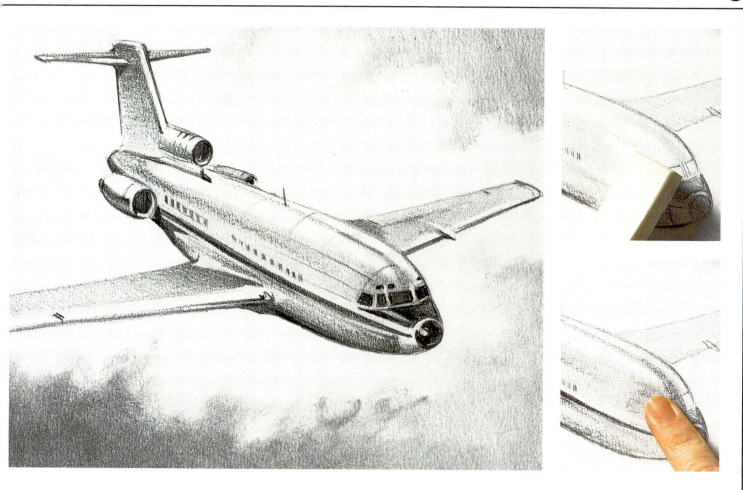

The finishing touches for your drawing consist of developing a range of contrasts and of blending with the stomp or your finger.

First, rub the sky between the clouds with the tip of the stomp.

Then, with a 2B pencil, add darker tones to the tail, motors, windows, and nose.

Last, use an eraser to bring out the highlights; finish blending with a finger the tones you previously graduated with the stomp.

My first exercises...

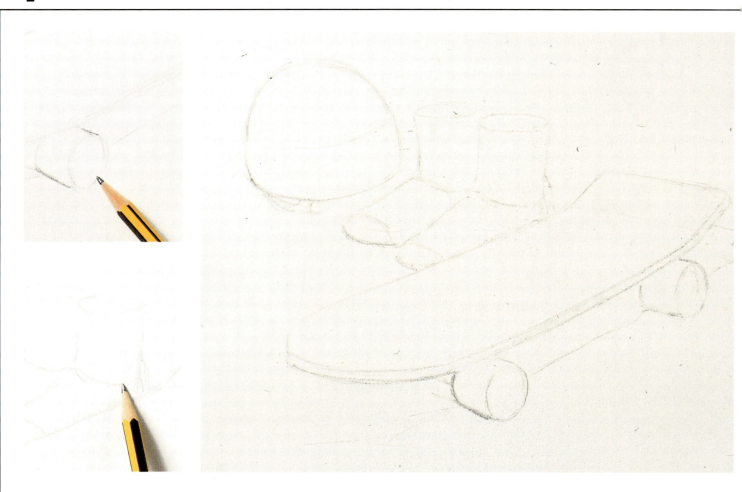

This exercise is done with a charcoal pencil. However, you may do your outline with a graphite pencil so you can erase and correct it without difficulty.

Charcoal lines, either from a stick or a pen-cil, are not easily erased, and marks always remain despite the use of an eraser. For this reason, don't outline your drawings with char-coal pencil until you have acquired more experience with this technique.

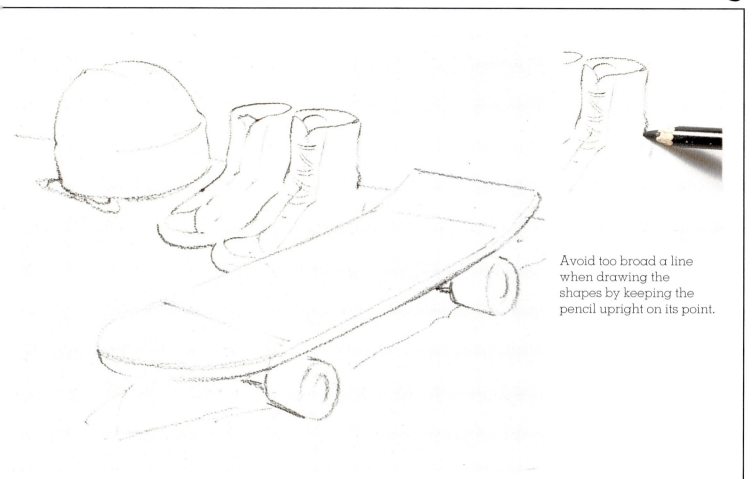

Avoid too broad a line when drawing the shapes by keeping the pencil upright on its point.

Once you have outlined and corrected your graphite pencil line, go over the lines again with your charcoal pencil.

Remember to work confidently and smoothly with the pencil, to avoid interrupted strokes.

After drawing the basic lines, add the details and shadows on the helmet and skateboard.

My first exercises...

Lean the pencil point on its broad side and add gray, using parallel strokes.

Draw some vertical strokes in the background behind the helmet and boots. Lay the broad side of the pencil point flat against the paper, bearing down with even pressure the entire time.

Draw diagonal strokes to develop the table surface. Press only lightly to obtain a light gray. Begin at the bottom right angle and decrease the pressure gradually as you proceed.

Draw the shadows on the helmet and, more intensely, under the skateboard.

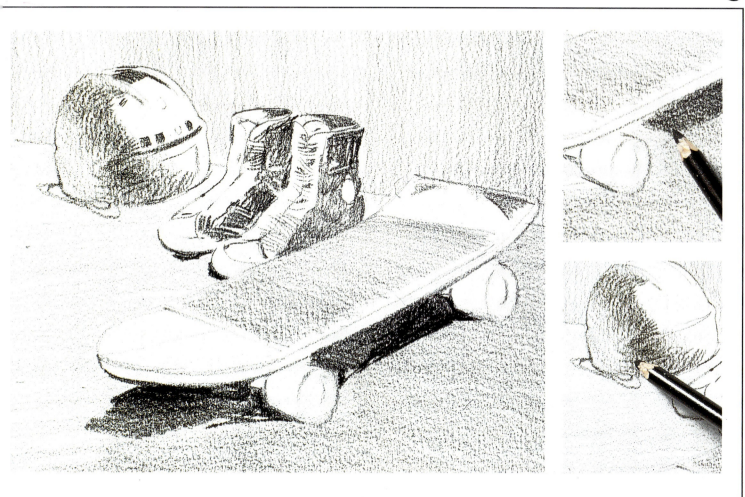

Intensify the shadows in this part of the exercise.

Add a gray to the top of the skateboard and a uniform background to each boot.

Next, draw cross-strokes, that is, strokes going in a different direction, over the gray of the helmet, boots, and the bottom right corner of the drawing.

Darken the shadow under the skateboard with repeated strokes.

My first exercises...

Draw a shadow on the wheel with parallel vertical strokes, and then intensify the strokes at the bottom of the wheel.

Now intensify some of the tones to blend them later with a stomp.

Do a gradation on the upper right and intensify the background behind the objects.

As you know, charcoal spreads readily, so keep your gradations short.

Add the designs at the ends of the board.

You must now blend the tones thoroughly with the stomp.

Blend the gradation you have created in the upper-right corner until it is a uniform gray.

Use the stomp to blend the shadows of the boots and helmet as well. Outline these shadows with fresh strokes.

Last, in the area next to the skateboard, darken the gray evenly with some cross-strokes and blend it with the stomp.

My first exercises...

The form of the locomotive can be first drawn in basic geometric shapes.

Your drawings can also have color.

Colored pencils and chalk—in particular sanguine chalk—are two of the materials you can use.

For this exercise, you will use only a san-guine chalk pencil to introduce you to its possibilities.

Use the chalk pencil as you would the charcoal and graphite pencils. First, draw some general tones like the locomotive's smoke and the foreground in front of the railroad tracks.

Add the parallel strokes on the train's engine.

Next, strengthen your preliminary outline and fill in the details.

My first exercises...

Give the cactus the first note of color, being careful not to go outside the outline.

In this part of the exercise, work mostly on the locomotive.

Give the boiler of the train's engine a uniform gray cast in the bottom part, then draw parallel strokes on its front part.

Do the same in the tender and the other car.

Intensify the strokes of the headlight, the smokestack, and the outlines of the boiler, but keep the sanguine chalk pencil perpendicular to the paper to obtain a fine line.

You now need to intensify a few tones to bring out the contrast in your drawing.

Start a gradation in the smokestack and the boiler of the locomotive, applying slightly more pressure on the chalk pencil at the beginning and progressively decreasing it.

In the front part of the locomotive, draw some parallel strokes; then, intensify the general tone of the area near the tracks and the cactus.

My first exercises...

Use the stomp as you have learned to do with the charcoal technique.

You must rub gently with the stomp over the sanguine chalk pencil strokes, to blend them.

Next, darken the bottom of the boiler and go over the outline of the drawing.

Redraw the outline with the fine point of the pencil.

Over a blended area, you can draw some strokes, as is done here in the smoke stream.

Let's give the last touches to our old locomotive.

With repeated strokes of the sanguine chalk pencil, try, most of all, to intensify the shadow areas to bring out the maximum contrast possible.

Now apply a few strokes, crossing them in a different direction, in the foreground, next to the tracks.

One last detail: draw the thorns on the cactus.

Glossary

beveled point. Angled or sloped edge on a pencil, whether graphite, charcoal, or chalk. It allows the drawing of fine and broad lines, depending on whether the edge or the flat sloped surface is used.

clay. A mineral substance, produced when certain rocks are broken down by the forces of water upon them. It is combined with graphite in the core of graphite pencils.

dimensions. The main measurements of a model or subject of a drawing.

fixative. A liquid that must be applied for setting the charcoal particles in a drawing, to prevent smudging. Fixative is available in spray cans from art supply stores.

form sketch. Preliminary lines in a drawing that set down the basic forms of a subject by means of simple geometric shapes (squares, rectangles, circles, etc.).

gradation. The gradual shift from a darker tone to a lighter one, or vice versa.

graphite. A soft carbon, with a greasy feel and metallic luster, combined with clay to manufacture the core of a graphite pencil. The amount of graphite in the core mixture determines the degree of hardness or softness of the pencil.

kneaded eraser. A soft pliable rubber substance that can be easily shaped to erase narrow areas. It can be cut up or kneaded to present a clean surface.

perspective. Drawing rules for creating on paper, which has only two dimensions (length and width), the impression of the third dimension (that is, depth).

proportions. The relationship between sizes of the different objects in a drawing. It is an important factor when drawing the preliminary outline.

sketch. A rough drawing in which the shape, composition, and tone intensities are determined.

sketchbook. A drawing pad especially reserved for notations or sketches that may later be used in a more formal drawing.

subject. The figure, object, or landscape that is the content of a drawing. It can be taken from life, from a photo or a printed illustration, or from another drawing.

Index